Table of Contents

Introduction 5
Brief overview of the uniqueness of "One Slam Wonders" and its significance in tennis history. 5
Highlighting the allure and challenges of winning a single Grand Slam. 8
Introducing Michael Chang, Tracy Austin, and Maria Bueno, setting the stage for their remarkable journeys. 11

Chapter 1: Michael Chang - A Teenage Sensation .. 16
Chang's Early Years 16
Rise to the French Open Triumph 19
The Impact of His Historic Victory 23
The Early Challenges: Injuries and Playing Style Changes 27

Chapter 2: Tracy Austin - A Teenage Prodigy 30
Austin's Tennis Genesis 30
The Record-Breaking US Open Triumph 33
Back Injury: A Cruel Twist of Fate 37
Battling to Regain Form 41

Chapter 3: Maria Bueno - Grace Under Pressure .. 45
Bueno's Tennis Roots 45
Triumph at the French Championships 48
The Onset of Injuries and Illness 52
The Fight for Consistency 56

Chapter 4: Struggles and Triumphs 59
How These Players Overcame Initial Setbacks 59
Chang's Resilience and Adaptation 63
Austin's Determination to Reclaim Success 67

Bueno's Valiant Efforts to Return to the Top 71
Chapter 5: Life Beyond Tennis 75
Chang's Transition and Post-Tennis Life 75
Austin's Career Beyond the Courts 79
Bueno's Impact on Tennis Legacy 83
Chapter 6: Legacy and Inspiration 86
The Lasting Impact of These One Slam Wonders 86
Lessons in Resilience and Determination 90
Inspiring Future Generations 94
Chapter 7: The Sporting World's Take 98
Insights and Quotes from Tennis Professionals and Experts 98
How These Players Are Remembered 102
Examining the Cultural and Historical Significance 106
Conclusion 110
Reflecting on the Journeys 110
The Unique Legacy of Michael Chang, Tracy Austin, and Maria Bueno 114
Leaving a Lasting Mark in Tennis History 118
Wordbook 122
Supplementary Materials 125

Copyright © 2023 by Ryan P. Parker (Author)

All rights reserved. No part of this book may be reproduced or utilized in any form or by any means, electronic or mechanical, including photocopying, recording or by any information storage and retrieval system, without permission in writing from the publisher, except for brief quotations in critical articles or reviews.

The content of this book is based on various sources and is intended for educational and entertainment purposes only. While the author has made every effort to ensure the accuracy, completeness, and reliability of the information provided, the information may be subject to errors, omissions, or inaccuracies. Therefore, the author makes no warranties, express or implied, regarding the content of this book.

Readers are advised to seek the guidance of a licensed professional before attempting any techniques or actions outlined in this book. The author is not responsible for any losses, damages, or injuries that may arise from the use of information contained within. The information provided in this book is not intended to be a substitute for professional advice, and readers should not rely solely on the information presented.

By reading this book, readers acknowledge that the author is not providing legal, financial, medical, or professional advice. Any reliance on the information contained in this book is solely at the reader's own risk.

Thank you for selecting this book as a valuable source of knowledge and inspiration. Our aim is to provide you with insights and information that will enrich your understanding and enhance your personal growth. We appreciate your decision to embark on this journey of discovery with us, and we hope that this book will exceed your expectations and leave a lasting impact on your life.

Title: Rising Stars and Stumbling Blocks
Subtitle: The Journeys of Michael Chang, Tracy Austin, and Maria Bueno

Series: Sports Through Time: A Comprehensive History
Author: Ryan P. Parker

Introduction

Brief overview of the uniqueness of "One Slam Wonders" and its significance in tennis history.

Tennis, like any other sport, has its legends and its lore. The annals of the game are brimming with names that resonate through the ages, etching themselves indelibly into the sport's storied history. Names like Roger Federer, Serena Williams, Rafael Nadal, and Martina Navratilova have dominated the courts for years, amassing Grand Slam titles and etching their legacies in the tennis pantheon. Yet, for every Federer, there exists a Michael Chang; for every Serena, a Tracy Austin; and for every Nadal, a Maria Bueno.

These are the "One Slam Wonders," an intriguing and often overlooked facet of tennis history. Unlike their more celebrated counterparts who have secured multiple Grand Slam victories, these remarkable athletes claimed the pinnacle of their sport on just one occasion. In the course of a single tournament, they transcended the limits of their abilities, defeated formidable opponents, and hoisted the coveted Grand Slam trophy. But, what sets them apart, what makes their stories so compelling, is not just the rarity of their achievement, but the journey they embarked upon afterward.

In this exploration of "One Slam Wonders," we delve into the captivating and often tumultuous stories of three remarkable individuals who, for that one shining moment, stood atop the tennis world: Michael Chang, Tracy Austin, and Maria Bueno. Their triumphs and tribulations serve as a testament to the unforgiving nature of professional sports and the enduring human spirit. Yet, their narratives transcend the confines of the tennis court, providing lessons in resilience, determination, and the indomitable will to surmount even the most formidable of challenges.

As we venture through the chapters that follow, we will witness the meteoric rise of these young talents, their struggles to maintain their position at the zenith of the sport, and their eventual transition into life beyond tennis. We will glean insights from tennis professionals, experts, and contemporaries, all of whom shed light on the cultural and historical significance of these "One Slam Wonders." Moreover, we will contemplate the lasting impact of these extraordinary individuals on the sport they loved and the inspiration they continue to provide to future generations of tennis enthusiasts.

Join us on this journey as we explore the unique world of "One Slam Wonders," a world where fleeting glory is transformed into lasting legacy, and where the pursuit of excellence is, in itself, an epic tale of courage and determination.

Highlighting the allure and challenges of winning a single Grand Slam.

In the world of tennis, the Grand Slam tournaments represent the pinnacle of achievement. The Australian Open, the French Open, Wimbledon, and the US Open—these hallowed grounds witness the clash of titans, where the finest athletes battle for supremacy on the global stage. Winning a Grand Slam is the ultimate aspiration for any tennis player, a singular moment that can define a career and secure a lasting legacy. But what about those who reach this summit only once, who savor the sweet taste of victory at one of these prestigious events and then must navigate the turbulent waters of expectation, injury, and competition? These are the "One Slam Wonders," a distinct breed of champions whose journeys both inspire and fascinate.

The Allure of a Grand Slam: Imagine the scene: a packed stadium bathed in sunlight, or perhaps under the glow of spotlights at night, the crowd's roars echoing through the air. At stake is not just a trophy, but immortality in the world of tennis. The allure of winning a Grand Slam is unparalleled—the sensation of holding that gleaming trophy aloft, of etching one's name alongside legends in the annals of the sport, and of standing on the podium as the world watches in awe. It's a dream that drives aspiring tennis players from all corners of the globe, propelling them to endure grueling training regimens, make personal sacrifices, and face the fierce competition that defines professional tennis.

A single Grand Slam victory is a testament to an athlete's skill, determination, and unwavering focus. It's a moment that validates years of relentless pursuit and dedication. For "One Slam Wonders," this moment of triumph is indescribable—an achievement that can never be taken away, a testament to their place among the tennis elite.

The Challenges of Staying on Top: Yet, as quickly as the triumph comes, so too do the challenges. Winning a Grand Slam is a monumental feat, but it is only the beginning of the journey. The world's gaze intensifies, expectations soar, and the pressure to replicate that success mounts. Maintaining the consistency required to dominate a sport as physically and mentally demanding as tennis is a herculean task. It demands not just talent, but the ability to withstand the physical toll of the game, the capriciousness of injuries, and the ever-evolving strategies of opponents who seek to dethrone the reigning champion.

For "One Slam Wonders," the challenge lies not only in conquering the tennis world but in holding onto their place at its summit. We'll delve into the stories of Michael

Chang, Tracy Austin, and Maria Bueno, individuals who tasted the sweetness of victory at a Grand Slam event and then grappled with the complexities of sustaining that success. Their journeys are marked by injuries that threatened to derail their careers, stylistic adaptations to stay competitive, and the emotional rollercoaster of striving to relive their moment of glory.

As we navigate the chapters that follow, we will dissect the allure and challenges of winning a single Grand Slam, delving deep into the stories of these remarkable "One Slam Wonders" to unearth the human drama, the triumphs, and the tribulations that define their place in tennis history.

Introducing Michael Chang, Tracy Austin, and Maria Bueno, setting the stage for their remarkable journeys.

In the vast tapestry of tennis history, certain names stand out as beacons of inspiration, their stories woven into the very fabric of the sport. Michael Chang, Tracy Austin, and Maria Bueno are three such luminous figures, each having etched their names in the annals of tennis in a unique and enduring manner. As we embark on this exploration of "One Slam Wonders," it is these three individuals who shall be our guides into the captivating realm of triumph and tribulation.

Michael Chang - A Teenage Sensation: Our journey begins with the remarkable tale of Michael Chang, a teenager whose audacity and determination defied the norms of professional tennis. Chang's story is a testament to youthful exuberance, unwavering faith, and the extraordinary capacity for resilience. In the heart of the tennis world, where seasoned veterans typically reigned, Chang emerged as an iconoclast. He redefined what it meant to be a young prodigy, challenging the established order and taking the tennis world by storm.

Chang's Early Years: We'll delve into Chang's formative years, tracing his tennis lineage and the influences that shaped his unorthodox style of play. From a young age, it was evident that this was no ordinary talent. His prodigious abilities were evident, but it was his determination and mental fortitude that truly set him apart.

Rise to the French Open Triumph: The crowning jewel of Chang's career came at the French Open, where he achieved a victory that would echo through tennis history. His triumph on the clay courts of Roland Garros was not just a victory of skill but also a triumph of willpower and tenacity that left the tennis world in awe.

The Impact of His Historic Victory: Chang's French Open victory was more than a mere Grand Slam win; it was a watershed moment that forever changed the perception of what young players could achieve in tennis. His courage in the face of adversity and his relentless pursuit of excellence continue to inspire generations of athletes.

The Early Challenges: Injuries and Playing Style Changes: However, Chang's journey was not without its share of challenges. The physical toll of the sport, coupled with the evolving strategies of his opponents, forced him to adapt and overcome. We'll explore the injuries he faced and the changes he made to his playing style to stay competitive.

Tracy Austin - A Teenage Prodigy: Transitioning from Chang's remarkable story, we turn our attention to Tracy

Austin, a teenage prodigy whose ascent in the world of tennis was nothing short of meteoric. Austin's journey is a tale of early success, a record-breaking triumph, and an unfortunate twist of fate that tested her resolve like never before.

Austin's Tennis Genesis: We'll uncover the origins of Austin's tennis career, from her early forays into the sport to the recognition of her extraordinary talent. Her rise in the tennis world was swift, marked by a precociousness that defied her age.

The Record-Breaking US Open Triumph: At the heart of Austin's narrative is her historic victory at the US Open, where she became the youngest Grand Slam champion in the history of the sport—a distinction that endures to this day. Her triumph was a moment of pure glory, a zenith that few athletes ever attain.

Back Injury: A Cruel Twist of Fate: But then came a cruel twist of fate—a debilitating back injury that threatened to extinguish her tennis dreams. We'll delve into Austin's harrowing battle to regain her form, a battle that tested her physical and mental resilience.

Battling to Regain Form: Austin's determination to return to the sport she loved, despite the odds stacked against her, is a testament to her indomitable spirit. Her journey serves as a poignant reminder of the fragility of success in the world of professional tennis.

Maria Bueno - Grace Under Pressure: Finally, we introduce Maria Bueno, a graceful and supremely talented athlete whose elegance on the court captivated tennis enthusiasts around the world. Bueno's journey is one marked by grace, precision, and the unrelenting pursuit of excellence, even in the face of adversity.

Bueno's Tennis Roots: We'll begin by tracing Bueno's tennis roots, her early influences, and the development of her signature style. Her finesse and elegance were a breath of fresh air in the competitive world of tennis.

Triumph at the French Championships: Bueno's moment of glory arrived at the French Championships, where she exhibited her mastery of the sport, claiming victory in stunning fashion. Her triumph was more than a win; it was a declaration of her artistry on the court.

The Onset of Injuries and Illness: However, as Bueno soared to the pinnacle of tennis, injuries and illness threatened to cast a shadow over her career. We'll explore the challenges she faced, both physical and personal, as she sought to maintain her position among the elite.

The Fight for Consistency: Bueno's quest for consistency in the face of adversity speaks to the enduring spirit of a champion. Her journey is a testament to the inner strength required to remain at the zenith of a sport that demands nothing short of perfection.

In the chapters that follow, we will navigate the intricate and inspiring journeys of these remarkable individuals, each of whom seized the pinnacle of their sport and then grappled with the complexities of sustaining their success. Their stories are testaments to the allure and challenges of winning a single Grand Slam, and they serve as beacons of inspiration for tennis enthusiasts and athletes alike.

Chapter 1: Michael Chang - A Teenage Sensation

Chang's Early Years

Before Michael Chang became a household name in the tennis world, before he astonished the sporting universe with his historic French Open triumph, there were the formative years—the years of dreams, dedication, and determination that set the stage for his remarkable journey.

A Tennis Prodigy in the Making

Michael Te-Pei Chang was born on February 22, 1972, in Hoboken, New Jersey, to Taiwanese immigrants Joe and Betty Chang. From a young age, it was evident that Michael possessed a natural affinity for sports. His early years were filled with athletic pursuits, and it wasn't long before tennis became his focal point.

The Chang family moved to Southern California, a tennis hotbed, where young Michael's talent began to blossom. He was introduced to the sport by his father, Joe, who recognized his son's potential and embarked on a mission to nurture that talent. The tennis courts of Palos Verdes became the backdrop for countless hours of practice and development. It was here that Chang's unique style of play began to take shape.

The Unconventional Style

What set Chang apart from his peers, even in those early years, was his unconventional playing style. While most young tennis players were groomed to overpower opponents with raw power, Chang's diminutive stature and quick footwork dictated a different approach. His father, Joe, encouraged him to develop a style that leveraged his agility and defensive skills, a style that would ultimately become his hallmark.

Chang's early years were marked by relentless drills and an unwavering commitment to perfecting his game. He displayed an uncanny ability to chase down seemingly impossible shots and return them with precision. His relentless work ethic and willingness to embrace a different path set him on a trajectory that would defy convention.

Emerging as a Junior Sensation

As Michael Chang entered the junior tennis circuit, it became evident that he was a force to be reckoned with. He quickly made a name for himself, not just for his on-court prowess but also for his sportsmanship and unassuming demeanor. Chang's humility and respect for the game endeared him to fans and fellow players alike.

In 1987, at the age of 15, Chang won the USTA Boys' 18s National Championship, making him the youngest player to do so in the tournament's history. It was a harbinger of the greatness that lay ahead, a glimpse of what he would achieve on the professional circuit.

Conclusion of Chang's Early Years

The early years of Michael Chang's life were marked by a relentless pursuit of tennis excellence. From his humble beginnings in New Jersey to the tennis courts of Southern California, he honed a playing style that defied convention. His emergence as a junior sensation was a testament to his talent, work ethic, and character.

As we journey deeper into the life of this remarkable athlete, we will witness the evolution of Michael Chang from a promising young talent into a tennis sensation. His early years provided the foundation for a career that would forever change the course of tennis history. In the chapters that follow, we will explore the rise of this teenage sensation and the pivotal moments that led to his historic victory at the French Open.

Rise to the French Open Triumph

In the annals of tennis history, the ascent of Michael Chang to the zenith of the sport remains a testament to youthful exuberance, unwavering faith, and the extraordinary capacity for resilience. It was a journey that began with humble roots and culminated in a momentous victory that would forever etch his name in the sport's history books—the French Open triumph of 1989.

Chang's Determination and Progression

As Michael Chang continued to make waves on the junior circuit, his determination and progression were evident to all who followed his burgeoning career. His unorthodox playing style, characterized by incredible speed and agility, was becoming increasingly difficult for opponents to counter. But it was not just his physical attributes that set him apart; it was also his mental fortitude and unwavering belief in himself.

Chang's early years on the professional circuit were marked by steady progress. He began to notch victories against more seasoned opponents, gradually making a name for himself. However, the French Open of 1989 would become the stage on which his true potential would be revealed.

The 1989 French Open: A Grand Slam Surprise

In May 1989, the tennis world turned its attention to Roland Garros, Paris, for the French Open. While the tennis elite vied for the prestigious title, a 17-year-old Michael Chang entered the tournament with a determined spirit and the belief that he could conquer the clay courts of Paris.

Chang's journey through the tournament was nothing short of extraordinary. He displayed not only his exceptional tennis skills but also his unshakable resolve. In the early rounds, he faced daunting opponents and grueling matches, often battling from behind. His remarkable fitness and ability to chase down shots became his defining traits, allowing him to outlast opponents and secure hard-fought victories.

The Semifinal Showdown with Lendl

As Chang advanced deeper into the tournament, he faced a formidable challenge in the semifinals—Ivan Lendl, a tennis titan and three-time defending French Open champion. Lendl was expected to breeze past the young American, but what ensued was a showdown that would go down in tennis lore.

Chang's tactics against Lendl were as unorthodox as they were effective. He employed an underhanded serve, a strategic move that disrupted Lendl's rhythm and rattled the experienced champion. It was a bold move that reflected

Chang's unwavering self-belief and willingness to do whatever it took to win.

In a stunning turn of events, Chang emerged victorious in a five-set thriller, defeating the world No. 1 and setting the stage for an improbable run to the French Open final.

The Final Triumph and Grand Slam Glory

In the final, Chang faced Stefan Edberg, another tennis great. The world watched with bated breath as the teenager from the United States took on the Swedish powerhouse. What transpired was a test of endurance, skill, and mental fortitude.

Chang's tenacity was on full display as he fought through a grueling match, eventually emerging victorious. In doing so, he became the youngest male player to win a Grand Slam title, a record that still stands to this day. The victory was not just a tennis achievement; it was a testament to the power of determination and the ability of the human spirit to conquer adversity.

Conclusion of the Rise to the French Open Triumph

Michael Chang's remarkable journey from a promising young talent to the winner of the 1989 French Open is a testament to his unwavering determination, unconventional style, and indomitable will. His triumph at

Roland Garros was more than a victory; it was a symbol of what can be achieved when talent, hard work, and belief in oneself converge.

In the chapters that follow, we will delve deeper into the impact of Chang's historic victory and the challenges he faced in maintaining his position at the pinnacle of tennis. His journey is a reminder that the allure of a single Grand Slam victory is only the beginning of a remarkable story.

The Impact of His Historic Victory

Michael Chang's triumphant run at the 1989 French Open was not merely a remarkable sporting achievement; it was a seismic event that resonated far beyond the tennis court. His historic victory transcended the boundaries of the sport and left an indelible mark on the world of athletics, inspiring generations to come.

Chang's French Open Triumph: A Defining Moment

The French Open final of 1989 was not just a tennis match; it was a moment of destiny for Michael Chang. His victory over Stefan Edberg was a testament to his extraordinary talent and unparalleled determination. As he held the coveted trophy aloft, he etched his name in the annals of tennis history and joined the pantheon of Grand Slam champions.

Chang's win was historic in several aspects. At 17 years and 110 days, he became the youngest male player to win a Grand Slam singles title—a record that endures to this day. His achievement was a symbol of youth triumphing over experience, of audacity prevailing over convention.

Inspiration to Aspiring Tennis Players

Michael Chang's French Open victory sent shockwaves through the tennis world, particularly among young and aspiring players. His improbable journey from an unseeded teenager to a Grand Slam champion became a source of inspiration for countless young athletes who dared to dream of greatness.

Tennis academies and coaches around the world began to emphasize the importance of mental fortitude, resilience, and unconventional tactics in their training regimens. Chang's underhanded serve, which had confounded opponents in that historic semifinal against Ivan Lendl, became a subject of discussion and experimentation among coaches and players alike.

Impact on Asian-American Representation

Chang's victory had profound cultural significance, particularly within the Asian-American community. As the first Asian-American male to win a Grand Slam singles title, he shattered stereotypes and blazed a trail for future generations. His triumph became a symbol of pride and achievement, showing that barriers could be broken and that success knew no boundaries of race or ethnicity.

Chang's success led to increased interest in tennis among Asian-American youth, and tennis clubs saw a surge in participation. His journey from the son of Taiwanese immigrants to a global sports icon demonstrated that talent and determination could transcend cultural backgrounds.

The Evolution of Tennis Tactics

Chang's unconventional style of play, characterized by speed, agility, and relentless defense, left an indelible mark on the sport's tactical landscape. Coaches and players began to reconsider the traditional power-focused approach to tennis, realizing that a well-rounded game that included elements of defense and counterattacking could be equally effective.

His use of drop shots, lobs, and baseline rallies as tools to outmaneuver opponents became a template for a new generation of players. The impact of Chang's victory was felt not only in the immediate aftermath but also in the evolution of tennis strategy in the years that followed.

Conclusion of The Impact of His Historic Victory

Michael Chang's triumph at the 1989 French Open was a watershed moment in tennis history, one that reverberated far beyond the confines of the court. His victory inspired aspiring tennis players, broke cultural barriers, and influenced the evolution of tennis tactics. It served as a testament to the power of determination, unconventional thinking, and unwavering self-belief.

As we delve deeper into the life and career of Michael Chang, we will explore the challenges he faced following his historic victory, including injuries and the changing landscape of professional tennis. His journey is a testament to the enduring allure and challenges of winning a single Grand Slam.

The Early Challenges: Injuries and Playing Style Changes

Michael Chang's ascent to tennis stardom was not without its share of trials and tribulations. Following his historic victory at the 1989 French Open, he confronted a new set of challenges that tested his resilience, adaptability, and determination to remain at the pinnacle of the sport.

Post-French Open Hurdles

After his stunning triumph at Roland Garros, Michael Chang returned to the professional circuit with heightened expectations and an increased level of scrutiny. The tennis world awaited his next move, eager to see if he could sustain the momentum generated by his historic victory.

However, as he navigated the post-French Open landscape, Chang encountered a series of early challenges that would shape the course of his career:

1. Physical Toll and Injuries:

One of the most immediate challenges that Chang faced was the physical toll of professional tennis. His playing style, characterized by relentless court coverage and exceptional defensive skills, placed immense strain on his body. Chang's diminutive stature made him susceptible to injuries, particularly to his lower limbs.

In the wake of his French Open win, he grappled with a series of injuries, including ankle sprains and knee issues. These setbacks disrupted his training and tournament schedule, and he found himself confronting the harsh reality of professional sports: the need to manage and overcome physical limitations.

2. Evolving Tennis Tactics:

The tennis landscape was also evolving in the early '90s. Opponents had dissected Chang's playing style and developed strategies to counteract his strengths. They sought to exploit his size and limitations by employing tactics that forced him into prolonged baseline rallies and tested his endurance.

Chang's reliance on defensive skills and counterpunching, which had served him well in his teenage years, faced new challenges as opponents adapted. He was forced to reevaluate his game and consider adjustments that would enable him to remain competitive at the highest level.

Adaptation and Resilience:

It was during these challenging times that Chang's character truly shone. His remarkable ability to adapt and his unwavering resilience became evident as he faced each hurdle head-on. He worked tirelessly to rehabilitate his injuries, often enduring grueling physical therapy sessions to get back on the court.

In response to the evolving tactics of his opponents, Chang embarked on a journey of tactical refinement. He began to incorporate a more offensive approach into his game, developing a more aggressive net game and refining his serve. These adjustments not only showcased his versatility as a player but also demonstrated his commitment to continuous improvement.

Conclusion of The Early Challenges: Injuries and Playing Style Changes

Michael Chang's journey was far from smooth sailing after his historic victory at the French Open. The early challenges he faced, both in terms of injuries and evolving tennis tactics, tested the very essence of his character. Yet, through determination, adaptation, and unwavering resolve, Chang proved that he was not merely a one-time wonder but a player capable of sustained success.

In the chapters that follow, we will explore how Chang continued to navigate the complexities of professional tennis, further cementing his place in the sport's history. His story is a testament to the enduring allure and challenges of winning a single Grand Slam, and his resilience continues to inspire aspiring athletes around the world.

Chapter 2: Tracy Austin - A Teenage Prodigy
Austin's Tennis Genesis

Before Tracy Austin became a household name in the world of tennis, before she achieved unprecedented success as a teenage prodigy, there were the early years—the genesis of her remarkable journey in the sport that would define her life.

A Tennis Family

Tracy Austin was born on December 12, 1962, in Palos Verdes Peninsula, California, into a family with deep-rooted connections to tennis. Her father, George Austin, was a former professional tennis player, and her mother, Jeanne, was a tennis coach. Tennis was not just a sport in the Austin household; it was a way of life.

From a very young age, Tracy was exposed to the game through her parents, who recognized her innate talent and passion for tennis. The family's home was adorned with tennis memorabilia and trophies, setting the stage for Tracy's future in the sport.

Early Days on the Court

Tracy's early days on the tennis court were marked by boundless enthusiasm and an insatiable desire to play and compete. She began hitting balls against the garage door at the age of two, displaying an uncanny hand-eye coordination that left her family in awe.

Her formal training commenced shortly thereafter under the watchful eyes of her parents. George and Jeanne Austin became Tracy's first coaches, instilling in her the fundamentals of the game. It was on the local courts of Southern California that Tracy's prodigious talent began to blossom. Her dedication to practice, combined with the expert guidance of her parents, paved the way for her rapid development as a tennis player.

The Junior Circuit Phenom

Tracy Austin's rise on the junior tennis circuit was nothing short of meteoric. She began competing in junior tournaments at an early age, and her success was immediate. Her dominance in the junior ranks was a harbinger of the greatness that lay ahead. Her aggressive baseline game and exceptional court coverage set her apart from her peers, making her a formidable opponent on any surface.

At the age of 12, Tracy Austin made history by becoming the youngest player to win a professional tournament match. Her victory over Heidi Eisterlehner at the 1975 Women's Tennis Association (WTA) event in Portland, Oregon, signaled her arrival as a prodigy of unparalleled promise.

Transition to the Professional Circuit

Tracy Austin's transition from the junior circuit to the professional ranks was a seamless one, marked by a maturity and poise that belied her age. Her parents continued to provide guidance and support, ensuring that she remained grounded amid the burgeoning fame and expectations.

In 1977, at the age of 14, Tracy Austin made her Grand Slam debut at the US Open. Her fearless approach and unwavering self-belief were on full display as she advanced to the quarterfinals, defeating several established players along the way. The tennis world had taken notice of this teenage phenom, and her journey had only just begun.

Conclusion of Austin's Tennis Genesis

The genesis of Tracy Austin's tennis journey was characterized by a family deeply rooted in the sport, early exposure to tennis, and a prodigious talent that manifested itself from a very young age. Her rapid ascent through the junior ranks and seamless transition to the professional circuit were early indicators of the remarkable career that awaited her.

As we delve deeper into the life and career of Tracy Austin, we will explore the challenges, triumphs, and unique qualities that defined her as a teenage prodigy and a prominent figure in the world of tennis.

The Record-Breaking US Open Triumph

In the annals of tennis history, Tracy Austin's ascent to stardom reached its zenith with her record-breaking victory at the US Open in 1979. At the age of 16, she achieved what many considered impossible, etching her name in the record books and securing her place as a teenage prodigy for the ages.

The 1979 US Open: A Grand Slam Showdown

The 1979 US Open was the stage for a remarkable showdown of tennis talent. The tournament attracted a formidable field of competitors, including established stars and seasoned veterans. At the center of this tennis spectacle was Tracy Austin, a teenage sensation with the world watching in anticipation.

Austin's Path to the Final:

Tracy's journey to the final was marked by tenacity and remarkable composure. She navigated the early rounds with precision, dispatching formidable opponents with a blend of power, finesse, and youthful exuberance. Her playing style, characterized by a relentless baseline game and exceptional shot placement, made her a force to be reckoned with on the hardcourts of Flushing Meadows.

In the semifinals, Austin faced off against Chris Evert, a tennis legend and multiple Grand Slam champion. The match was a grueling test of wills, with Tracy ultimately triumphing in a marathon three-set battle. Her victory over Evert signaled her readiness to seize the coveted US Open title.

The Final Showdown with Navratilova:

In the final, Tracy Austin met Martina Navratilova, another tennis icon known for her power and versatility. The world watched with bated breath as these two formidable players clashed on the grandest stage of American tennis.

The final was a masterclass in tennis prowess. Tracy's ability to control rallies, dictate play, and unleash powerful groundstrokes was on full display. Her unwavering focus and competitive spirit were evident as she took the first set. Navratilova, however, mounted a spirited comeback, setting the stage for an epic battle.

In a tense and thrilling contest, Tracy Austin held her nerve and emerged victorious, clinching the US Open title. At 16 years and 9 months, she became the youngest player in history to win the US Open—a record that endures to this day.

Record-Breaking Impact:

Tracy Austin's victory at the 1979 US Open was a record-breaking achievement that captured the world's attention. Her status as the youngest-ever Grand Slam champion marked her as a tennis prodigy of unparalleled promise. Her victory not only shattered age-related records but also cemented her place in tennis history.

Legacy and Inspiration:

Tracy Austin's triumph at the US Open left an indelible mark on the sport. Her youthful exuberance, technical prowess, and unwavering determination served as an inspiration to aspiring tennis players worldwide. Her story resonated with young athletes who dared to dream big and believe in their abilities.

Austin's victory also highlighted the potential of young athletes to compete at the highest level of professional sports. Her success challenged the conventional wisdom that tennis excellence was reserved for seasoned players and signaled a shift in the sport's dynamics.

Conclusion of The Record-Breaking US Open Triumph:

Tracy Austin's record-breaking victory at the 1979 US Open was a defining moment in tennis history. Her remarkable journey from a tennis prodigy to the youngest Grand Slam champion was a testament to her skill, determination, and remarkable poise under pressure. Her legacy would extend far beyond the court, inspiring future generations of tennis players and setting new standards for what young athletes could achieve in the world of professional sports.

As we delve deeper into the life and career of Tracy Austin, we will explore the challenges she faced following this historic victory and her enduring impact on the world of tennis. Her story continues to inspire and resonate with tennis enthusiasts and athletes alike.

Back Injury: A Cruel Twist of Fate

Tracy Austin's meteoric rise in the world of tennis was marked not only by her astounding successes but also by the challenges that tested her resolve and resilience. Among these challenges, none was more significant and cruel than the back injury that threatened to derail her promising career.

The Aftermath of Triumph:

In the wake of her historic victory at the 1979 US Open, Tracy Austin stood on the cusp of tennis greatness. The tennis world had witnessed the emergence of a teenage prodigy with immense talent and poise. Expectations were high, and her future seemed boundless.

However, the life of a professional athlete is fraught with physical demands and intense competition. Tracy's rigorous training and relentless playing schedule took a toll on her young body, particularly her lower back. It was a part of her anatomy that would soon become the focal point of her career's most formidable challenge.

The Onset of Back Troubles:

The first signs of trouble appeared in 1980 when Tracy began experiencing persistent back pain. Initially dismissed as routine aches and strains, the discomfort soon intensified, affecting her mobility and performance on the court. For a player whose game relied on agility and quick court coverage, the back injury was a devastating blow.

Tracy sought medical advice and embarked on a regimen of rest and rehabilitation. It was a frustrating period marked by uncertainty and a longing to return to the sport she loved. Her hiatus from competitive tennis was a harsh reminder of the fragility of athletic success.

The Comeback Attempt:

Tracy's determination to return to professional tennis was unwavering. She undertook a careful and deliberate recovery process, working with physical therapists, trainers, and medical experts to rehabilitate her back. The road to recovery was grueling, marked by countless hours of rehabilitation exercises and cautious optimism.

In 1981, after nearly a year of rehabilitation, Tracy Austin made her comeback to competitive tennis. Her return was met with anticipation and hope from fans who had followed her journey. The tennis world watched with keen interest as she resumed her professional career, eager to witness the resurgence of the teenage prodigy.

A Return to Grand Slam Glory:

Tracy's triumphant return culminated in a remarkable achievement at the 1981 US Open. Against the odds and after overcoming a debilitating back injury, she clinched her second Grand Slam title, reaffirming her status as one of the sport's most talented and resilient players.

Her victory at the US Open was a testament to her unwavering spirit and determination. It was a poignant moment in her career, one that showcased her ability to overcome adversity and rise to the pinnacle of the sport.

The Lingering Impact:

Despite her successful return, Tracy Austin's back injury continued to plague her throughout her career. The physical toll of professional tennis, coupled with the demands of rehabilitation and maintenance, became a constant presence in her life.

The back injury, while cruel and disruptive, also served to underscore Tracy's remarkable character. Her ability to persevere through pain and adversity endeared her to fans and fellow athletes alike. Her story became an inspiration to those who faced physical setbacks, proving that the human spirit could conquer even the most formidable challenges.

Conclusion of Back Injury: A Cruel Twist of Fate:

Tracy Austin's battle with a debilitating back injury was a defining chapter in her career. It tested her resilience, determination, and love for the sport. Her triumphant return to Grand Slam glory was a testament to her indomitable spirit, proving that even in the face of adversity, a teenage prodigy could rise above and leave an enduring mark in the world of tennis.

As we continue to explore Tracy Austin's remarkable journey, we will delve into her post-injury career, her impact on the sport, and the lessons in perseverance and resilience that her story imparts to athletes and enthusiasts around the world.

Battling to Regain Form

Tracy Austin's triumphant return to the world of professional tennis after her back injury was a testament to her unwavering determination and resilience. However, the road to regaining her form and reclaiming her position among the tennis elite was fraught with challenges that would test her resolve and determination.

The Comeback Trail:

After her successful return to competitive tennis in 1981, Tracy Austin embarked on a journey to regain her peak form. Her hiatus from the sport, coupled with the grueling rehabilitation process, had taken a toll on her game. She recognized that to compete at the highest level once again, she needed to rediscover her rhythm and hone her skills.

Tracy approached her comeback with a steely determination. She worked tirelessly on the practice courts, refining her strokes, and rebuilding her match fitness. Her relentless commitment to improvement became a source of inspiration for fellow athletes and fans alike.

Challenges on the Court:

The challenges Tracy faced on her path to regaining form were not limited to physical fitness alone. The mental aspect of her game was equally crucial. The fear of reinjury loomed large, casting a shadow over her every move on the court. She had to confront the psychological hurdles that came with the knowledge of what her body had endured.

Tracy's competitive spirit and mental toughness shone through as she navigated these challenges. She sought the guidance of sports psychologists to help her overcome the mental barriers that often accompany injuries. Her ability to channel her fears and doubts into a renewed sense of purpose became a hallmark of her comeback.

Return to Grand Slam Contention:

Tracy Austin's journey to regain form was punctuated by key moments of triumph and heartache. She returned to Grand Slam contention, but the path was arduous. Despite facing younger and increasingly powerful opponents, Tracy's tactical acumen and court craft allowed her to remain competitive.

In 1982, she reached the semifinals of the US Open, signaling her resurgence as a top-tier player. Her performance was a testament to her tenacity and the enduring quality of her game. Tracy's ability to compete at the highest level after a debilitating injury was a source of inspiration to athletes around the world.

Challenges Beyond the Court:

Tracy's journey to regain form extended beyond the confines of the tennis court. She grappled with the pressures of expectations and the scrutiny that came with her return. The media and fans closely monitored her every move, eager to witness her resurgence. Managing these external pressures while focusing on her comeback was a skill Tracy honed with time and experience.

Legacy of Resilience:

Tracy Austin's battle to regain form was a testament to her resilience and unwavering commitment to the sport she loved. Her story serves as a source of inspiration to athletes who face setbacks and challenges in their careers. Her ability to confront adversity head-on and emerge stronger serves as a reminder that even the most daunting obstacles can be overcome through determination and perseverance.

Conclusion of Battling to Regain Form:

Tracy Austin's journey to regain her form after a debilitating back injury was a testament to her resilience, mental fortitude, and enduring love for tennis. Her comeback showcased her ability to overcome not only physical setbacks but also the psychological and emotional challenges that accompany injuries.

As we continue to explore Tracy Austin's remarkable career, we will delve into her later achievements, her impact on the sport, and the enduring legacy of a teenage prodigy who refused to be defined by adversity.

Chapter 3: Maria Bueno - Grace Under Pressure
Bueno's Tennis Roots

Before Maria Bueno became an international tennis icon known for her elegance and grace on the court, there were the formative years—the roots of her extraordinary journey in the world of tennis.

Early Years in São Paulo:

Maria Esther Bueno was born on October 11, 1939, in São Paulo, Brazil. Her early exposure to tennis came through her father, Pedro Bueno, who was a prominent figure in Brazilian tennis circles. The Bueno family's love for the sport ran deep, and it was amidst this tennis-centric environment that Maria's passion for the game took root.

Maria's childhood was marked by countless hours spent on the tennis court, honing her skills under her father's watchful eye. The clay courts of São Paulo became her second home, and it was here that she began to develop the fundamentals that would later define her as a player.

The Rise Through Junior Tennis:

Maria Bueno's talent and potential became evident at a young age. Her natural ability to strike the ball with precision and her exceptional hand-eye coordination set her apart from her peers. As a junior player, she quickly ascended through the ranks, garnering attention for her remarkable skills and competitive spirit.

In 1955, at the age of 15, Maria captured her first national championship in Brazil, signaling her arrival as a tennis prodigy. Her success on the national stage provided a glimpse of the international acclaim that awaited her.

The Transition to the International Stage:

Maria Bueno's transition from the Brazilian tennis circuit to the international arena was a significant step in her burgeoning career. Her breakthrough on the global stage came in 1957 when she won the Wimbledon Girls' Singles Championship. Her victory at the prestigious tournament marked the beginning of a remarkable journey that would see her become a dominant force in women's tennis.

The Impact of Bueno's Style:

Maria Bueno's playing style was characterized by elegance, precision, and an artistic flair that set her apart from her contemporaries. She possessed a graceful one-handed backhand and exquisite shot-making ability, often leaving spectators in awe of her talent. Her ability to dictate rallies and employ a variety of shots made her a formidable opponent on any surface.

Bueno's style transcended the boundaries of sports; it was a fusion of athleticism and artistry. Her approach to the game was a source of inspiration not only to aspiring tennis players but also to those who appreciated the beauty of the sport.

Legacy of Brazilian Tennis:

Maria Bueno's impact on Brazilian tennis was profound and enduring. She became a national hero and a symbol of pride for her country. Her success inspired generations of Brazilian tennis players, encouraging them to dream big and pursue excellence on the international stage.

Bueno's achievements also raised the profile of tennis in Brazil, paving the way for future talent and the growth of the sport in the country. Her legacy as a trailblazer and ambassador for Brazilian tennis continues to influence the sport's development in Brazil.

Conclusion of Bueno's Tennis Roots:

Maria Bueno's tennis roots in São Paulo, Brazil, were the foundation upon which her remarkable career was built. Her early exposure to the sport, natural talent, and unwavering determination laid the groundwork for her ascent to tennis greatness. In the chapters that follow, we will explore the challenges and triumphs that defined Bueno's journey and her enduring impact on the world of tennis.

Triumph at the French Championships

Maria Bueno's journey to tennis greatness reached a pinnacle with her historic victory at the French Championships, a triumph that would solidify her reputation as one of the sport's most elegant and accomplished players.

The French Championships: A Prestigious Grand Slam:

The French Championships, now known as the French Open, has long been regarded as one of the most prestigious events in the tennis calendar. Its distinctive red clay courts pose unique challenges to players, demanding exceptional adaptability and court craft.

In the late 1950s, as Maria Bueno's star continued to rise, the French Championships beckoned as the ultimate test of her abilities. It was on these hallowed grounds that she would etch her name in tennis history.

Bueno's Journey to the Final:

The road to the 1959 French Championships final was marked by exceptional performances and a display of Bueno's unparalleled prowess on clay. Her elegant and fluid playing style found a perfect match on the slow, demanding surface.

Maria's path to the final was characterized by her ability to outmaneuver opponents, employ a wide array of shots, and adapt her game to the unique challenges posed by clay. Her remarkable backhand, delicate drop shots, and impeccable shot placement became her weapons of choice on the red dirt of Roland Garros.

The Epic Final Showdown:

In the final of the 1959 French Championships, Maria Bueno faced the formidable Margaret Smith, later known as Margaret Court, a fellow tennis legend. The stage was set for a memorable showdown between two of the sport's greatest talents.

The final was a masterclass in tennis artistry. Bueno's elegant strokes and Court's powerful game clashed in a battle of contrasting styles. The match was marked by long rallies, exceptional shot-making, and moments of sheer brilliance.

In a closely contested encounter, Maria Bueno displayed nerves of steel and an unyielding determination. She emerged victorious, defeating Court to capture her first French Championships title. Her victory was historic, making her the first South American woman to win the prestigious event.

The Significance of the Victory:

Maria Bueno's triumph at the 1959 French Championships was significant on multiple fronts. It established her as a versatile player capable of conquering different playing surfaces, silencing any doubts about her clay-court prowess.

Her victory also marked a breakthrough for South American tennis, inspiring a new generation of players from the region to aim for Grand Slam success. Bueno's achievements shattered geographical barriers and showcased the global reach of the sport.

Bueno's Elegance and Grace:

Maria Bueno's playing style was characterized by its elegance and grace. Her fluid movements on the court, combined with her impeccable timing, made her a joy to watch. She brought an artistic quality to tennis, captivating fans and earning admiration from fellow players.

Bueno's victory at the French Championships underscored her ability to win not only with power but also with finesse and precision. Her legacy as a player who elevated the aesthetics of tennis endured long after her retirement.

Conclusion of Triumph at the French Championships:

Maria Bueno's triumph at the 1959 French Championships was a crowning achievement in her illustrious career. It showcased her adaptability, versatility, and exceptional tennis artistry. Her victory not only added another Grand Slam title to her name but also left an indelible mark on the sport, reminding us of the enduring appeal of elegance and grace in tennis.

As we continue to explore Maria Bueno's remarkable journey, we will delve into her life beyond tennis, her impact on the sport's legacy, and the enduring grace that defined her on and off the court.

The Onset of Injuries and Illness

Maria Bueno's tennis journey, though filled with remarkable successes, was not without its share of challenges. In this chapter, we explore a period in her career marked by the onset of injuries and illness, testing her resilience and determination.

The Physical Demands of Professional Tennis:

As Maria Bueno continued to compete at the highest levels of professional tennis, the physical demands of the sport took a toll on her body. The rigorous training, relentless travel, and the strain of competitive play began to manifest in the form of injuries and health setbacks.

In the early 1960s, Bueno faced a series of injuries, including nagging knee issues and back problems. These physical setbacks disrupted her training and tournament schedule, forcing her to confront the challenges of maintaining peak performance in a sport that demanded nothing less.

The Mental Toll:

For a player of Bueno's caliber, who had tasted the sweet victory of Grand Slam titles, grappling with injuries and illness was as much a mental battle as a physical one. The fear of not being able to play at her best and the frustration of watching opportunities slip away weighed heavily on her psyche.

During this period, Maria Bueno also faced personal trials that added to her mental burden. The combination of physical and emotional challenges presented an enormous test of her mental fortitude.

Battling Illness:

In addition to injuries, Bueno's career was further complicated by health issues. In the mid-1960s, she was diagnosed with a serious illness that required extensive medical treatment and recovery. The diagnosis and treatment process were shrouded in uncertainty, and Bueno faced the prospect of an extended absence from the sport she loved.

Her battle with illness tested not only her physical strength but also her resilience and determination to return to competitive tennis. Bueno's journey was marked by countless hours of rehabilitation, setbacks, and moments of doubt.

The Comeback and Triumph Over Adversity:

Despite the challenges posed by injuries and illness, Maria Bueno's competitive spirit remained undiminished. Her tenacity and determination led to a remarkable comeback in the late 1960s. She defied the odds and returned to competitive tennis, displaying the same grace and skill that had defined her earlier career.

In 1968, she clinched her final Grand Slam title, the Wimbledon Women's Doubles, in partnership with Margaret Court. Her victory was a testament to her enduring passion for the sport and her ability to triumph over adversity.

The Legacy of Resilience:

Maria Bueno's battle with injuries and illness showcased her resilience and unwavering commitment to tennis. Her ability to overcome physical and mental setbacks stands as a testament to her character and determination.

Her story continues to inspire athletes who face injuries and health challenges, serving as a reminder that the human spirit can overcome even the most daunting obstacles. Bueno's legacy is not just one of triumph on the tennis court but also a story of unwavering grace and resilience in the face of adversity.

Conclusion of The Onset of Injuries and Illness:

Maria Bueno's journey through injuries and illness was a defining chapter in her illustrious career. It was a period marked by physical and mental challenges, but it was also a testament to her resilience and determination. Her ability to confront setbacks and return to the sport she loved underscores the enduring spirit of a tennis icon who faced adversity with grace under pressure.

As we continue to explore Maria Bueno's remarkable life and career, we will delve into her post-tennis contributions, her enduring impact on the sport, and the legacy she leaves for future generations.

The Fight for Consistency

Maria Bueno's tennis career was marked by incredible highs, but it was also characterized by the relentless pursuit of consistency—a battle that tested her dedication and resolve as she aimed to maintain her place among the tennis elite.

The Challenge of Sustained Success:

After her triumphant victory at the 1959 French Championships, Maria Bueno faced the challenge of sustaining her success on the international stage. The expectations placed upon her were substantial, and the world watched as she endeavored to prove that her Grand Slam win was not an isolated triumph but the beginning of a legendary career.

The journey towards consistency required Bueno to continue refining her game, adapting to changes in the sport, and competing against a new generation of talented players who sought to dethrone the reigning champion.

Battles on Multiple Fronts:

As Bueno pursued consistency, she encountered various obstacles that tested her mettle. The physical demands of professional tennis continued to take their toll, and injuries remained an ever-present threat. Maintaining peak fitness and health became an ongoing challenge.

Moreover, the mental aspect of the sport played a pivotal role in her quest for consistency. The pressure of being a defending champion, the scrutiny from fans and media, and the weight of personal expectations all required a mental fortitude that matched her physical prowess.

Adapting to Changing Styles:

Tennis, like any sport, evolves over time. New playing styles, strategies, and equipment advancements continually shape the landscape of the game. For Bueno, staying competitive meant adapting her classic and graceful playing style to contend with the power-based approaches of emerging players.

Bueno's ability to adapt her game without compromising her elegance and finesse was a testament to her skill and versatility. She embraced change as a means to maintain her edge in an ever-evolving sport.

The Pursuit of Additional Grand Slam Titles:

Maria Bueno's pursuit of consistency was intrinsically tied to her desire to add more Grand Slam titles to her resume. She continued to compete at the highest level, vying for championships at Wimbledon, the US Open, and the Australian Open.

Her journey included several close calls and hard-fought battles, as she sought to capture additional major titles. The quest for consistency was a quest for more moments of glory on the biggest stages in tennis.

Legacy of a Fighter:

Maria Bueno's fight for consistency was a testament to her spirit and determination. Her ability to contend with injuries, adapt to changes in the sport, and remain a competitive force showcased her unwavering commitment to tennis.

Her legacy extends beyond the trophies and titles she amassed. Bueno's story serves as a source of inspiration to athletes who strive for excellence and consistency in the face of adversity. Her graceful and relentless pursuit of tennis greatness left an indelible mark on the sport.

Conclusion of The Fight for Consistency:

Maria Bueno's battle for consistency was a defining aspect of her illustrious tennis career. Her journey to maintain her place among the tennis elite was marked by physical and mental challenges, adaptation to changing playing styles, and a relentless pursuit of Grand Slam titles.

As we continue to explore Maria Bueno's remarkable life and career, we will delve into her lasting contributions to the sport, her impact on the world of tennis, and the enduring legacy she leaves for future generations.

Chapter 4: Struggles and Triumphs
How These Players Overcame Initial Setbacks

The journeys of Michael Chang, Tracy Austin, and Maria Bueno were not without their fair share of setbacks and challenges. In this chapter, we delve into how these remarkable individuals overcame their initial obstacles, setting the stage for their enduring triumphs in the world of tennis.

The Power of Resilience:

Resilience is a common thread that runs through the stories of Michael Chang, Tracy Austin, and Maria Bueno. Each of them faced setbacks early in their careers that could have derailed their paths to success. Instead, they used these setbacks as opportunities to grow stronger and more determined.

Chang's Early Struggles:

Michael Chang's journey as a teenage sensation was not without its early challenges. His relatively small stature led to doubts about his ability to compete with taller and more powerful opponents. In his early years on the tour, he often found himself overpowered by stronger players.

However, Chang's tenacity and exceptional work ethic became his greatest assets. He embarked on a physical conditioning regimen that focused on building strength and endurance. His determination to overcome his physical limitations allowed him to compete at the highest level and ultimately win the French Open.

Austin's Battle with Injuries:

Tracy Austin's career was marked by significant injuries, particularly her back injury. After her historic US Open victory, she faced doubts about her ability to recover fully and return to her winning ways.

Austin's journey back to the top of the tennis world was marked by meticulous rehabilitation and a relentless desire to regain her form. She worked with sports psychologists to overcome the mental hurdles that came with injury, and her commitment to her craft allowed her to achieve sustained success on the tour.

Bueno's Health Challenges:

Maria Bueno's career was impacted by both injuries and illness. Her physical setbacks, combined with a life-threatening illness, could have derailed her tennis ambitions. However, Bueno's fighting spirit and unwavering determination enabled her to overcome these health challenges and continue competing at a high level.

Her ability to adapt her game to accommodate her physical condition was a testament to her skill and versatility as a player. Bueno's determination to pursue excellence in the face of adversity became a source of inspiration for her fellow athletes and fans around the world.

The Role of Support Systems:

All three players benefited from strong support systems that played pivotal roles in their comebacks. Whether it was the guidance of experienced coaches, the encouragement of family and friends, or the expertise of sports psychologists and medical professionals, these support networks provided crucial assistance during their times of struggle.

The Resilience of Champions:

The stories of Michael Chang, Tracy Austin, and Maria Bueno serve as reminders that champions are not defined solely by their victories but by their ability to rebound from setbacks. Their journeys are a testament to the power of resilience, determination, and the human spirit's ability to overcome adversity.

Conclusion of How These Players Overcame Initial Setbacks:

The early setbacks faced by Michael Chang, Tracy Austin, and Maria Bueno could have discouraged lesser individuals from pursuing their dreams in tennis. Instead, these remarkable players used adversity as a stepping stone to greater heights. Their stories serve as enduring examples of how resilience and determination can lead to triumph in the world of sports and beyond.

As we delve further into their careers and legacies, we will uncover more inspiring chapters in the lives of these tennis icons who refused to let initial setbacks define their destinies.

Chang's Resilience and Adaptation

Michael Chang's journey to becoming a tennis legend was characterized by remarkable resilience and an unwavering commitment to adapt and overcome the challenges he faced throughout his career.

The Early Years: A Budding Tennis Prodigy:

Michael Chang's tennis journey began at a young age, and his prodigious talent was evident from the start. He showed exceptional promise, marked by his agility, speed, and remarkable court coverage. His early success in junior tournaments signaled his potential as a future tennis star.

However, as Chang transitioned to the professional circuit, he faced formidable obstacles that threatened to impede his progress. Standing at just 5 feet 9 inches tall, he was often seen as undersized compared to many of his opponents. His relatively small stature led to doubts about his ability to compete effectively at the highest level of tennis.

The French Open Triumph: A Historic Achievement:

Despite the skepticism surrounding his size, Michael Chang's defining moment came at the 1989 French Open. At the age of 17, he embarked on a historic run at Roland Garros, capturing the hearts of tennis fans around the world.

In a tournament marked by grit and determination, Chang demonstrated an uncanny ability to outlast his opponents in physically demanding matches. His marathon victory over Ivan Lendl in the fourth round, where he famously employed an underhanded serve on crucial points, showcased his mental resilience and tactical adaptability.

Chang's triumph at the French Open was not only a historic achievement but also a testament to his ability to adapt his game to overcome seemingly insurmountable odds.

The Physical and Mental Resilience:

One of Michael Chang's greatest strengths was his relentless work ethic and commitment to physical conditioning. Despite his smaller frame, he focused on building strength and endurance to compete effectively against more powerful opponents.

Chang's mental resilience was equally remarkable. He possessed a steely resolve that allowed him to thrive in pressure-filled situations. He remained composed and mentally tough in critical moments, a quality that set him apart on the tennis court.

Adapting to Changing Playing Styles:

As the tennis landscape evolved, Michael Chang faced the challenge of adapting to the changing playing styles of his competitors. He encountered players with powerful serves and baseline games that posed unique challenges to his defensive style of play.

Chang's ability to adapt his game to counter these challenges demonstrated his versatility as a player. He developed a well-rounded game that included an improved serve, aggressive net play, and strategic shot-making, allowing him to remain competitive against a new generation of tennis talents.

Legacy of Resilience and Adaptation:

Michael Chang's career is a testament to the power of resilience and adaptability in the world of professional sports. He showed that success in tennis is not solely determined by physical attributes but also by mental toughness, dedication, and the willingness to evolve as a player.

His story continues to inspire aspiring tennis players and athletes across the globe, reminding them that with the right mindset and unwavering determination, one can overcome even the most formidable challenges and leave an enduring legacy in the world of sports.

Conclusion of Chang's Resilience and Adaptation:

Michael Chang's journey from a young tennis prodigy to a Grand Slam champion is a testament to his remarkable resilience and adaptability. His ability to overcome doubts about his size, his historic French Open triumph, and his ongoing commitment to physical and mental conditioning showcase the qualities that define a true champion.

As we continue to explore the lives and careers of tennis icons like Michael Chang, Tracy Austin, and Maria Bueno, we uncover the enduring stories of individuals who refused to be defined by their challenges, using them as stepping stones to greatness in the world of tennis.

Austin's Determination to Reclaim Success

Tracy Austin's tennis journey was marked by remarkable determination, resilience, and a fierce desire to reclaim success in the face of significant setbacks and challenges.

A Teenage Prodigy's Early Success:

Tracy Austin's rise to prominence in women's tennis began at an astonishingly young age. By the age of 14, she had already captured the attention of the tennis world, becoming the youngest player to win a professional tournament. Her meteoric ascent continued with her historic victory at the 1979 US Open, where she became the youngest Grand Slam champion.

However, the early success that catapulted her into the tennis spotlight was accompanied by heightened expectations, pressure, and the physical toll of professional tennis. These factors set the stage for the challenges that lay ahead.

The Cruel Twist of Fate: A Career-Threatening Injury:

One of the most defining moments in Tracy Austin's career was the unfortunate back injury she sustained in 1980. The injury, which occurred in a car accident, had the potential to derail her tennis ambitions and cast doubt on her ability to return to the top of the sport.

Austin's determination to overcome this career-threatening setback was unwavering. She embarked on a grueling rehabilitation journey, working tirelessly with physical therapists and medical professionals to regain her health and strength. Her determination to heal and reclaim her place on the tennis court was fueled by a relentless drive to succeed.

The Psychological Battle: Overcoming Doubt and Fear:

Recovery from a serious injury is not just a physical battle but also a mental one. Tracy Austin faced moments of doubt and fear as she contemplated her return to competitive tennis. The fear of reinjury and the uncertainty of whether she could recapture her form weighed heavily on her mind.

Austin's mental fortitude and determination were evident as she confronted these psychological challenges head-on. She sought the guidance of sports psychologists to develop strategies for managing anxiety and maintaining a positive mindset. Her ability to conquer her inner demons became a hallmark of her comeback.

Return to Grand Slam Contention: A Remarkable Comeback:

Tracy Austin's remarkable comeback to competitive tennis was marked by her unyielding spirit and a string of impressive performances. She defied the odds by reaching the finals of the 1981 US Open, announcing her return to Grand Slam contention in dramatic fashion.

Her journey back to the top was characterized by an improved game, adaptability, and a renewed sense of purpose. Austin's ability to compete at the highest level of women's tennis after a devastating injury was an inspiration to athletes worldwide.

Legacy of Determination:

Tracy Austin's determination to reclaim success serves as a testament to the power of resilience and unwavering commitment in the world of sports. Her story continues to inspire athletes who face setbacks and challenges in their careers, reminding them that with dedication and the right mindset, they can overcome even the most formidable obstacles.

Austin's legacy extends beyond her Grand Slam victories; it is a story of relentless determination, inner strength, and the refusal to be defined by adversity.

Conclusion of Austin's Determination to Reclaim Success:

Tracy Austin's journey from a teenage prodigy to a Grand Slam champion and her subsequent comeback from a career-threatening injury is a tale of unyielding determination and unwavering commitment. Her ability to overcome doubt, fear, and physical setbacks exemplifies the resilience that defines a true champion.

As we continue to explore the lives and careers of tennis icons like Tracy Austin, Michael Chang, and Maria Bueno, we uncover stories of individuals who refused to surrender to the challenges they faced, using them as stepping stones to triumph in the world of tennis.

Bueno's Valiant Efforts to Return to the Top

Maria Bueno's tennis journey was marked by incredible grace, resilience, and an indomitable spirit that allowed her to navigate the challenges of injuries and illness and make a valiant effort to return to the pinnacle of the sport.

The Impact of Injuries and Illness:

As we explored earlier, Maria Bueno faced a series of injuries and health setbacks that disrupted her tennis career. These challenges were not merely physical; they tested her mental fortitude and determination to continue competing at the highest level.

Bueno's journey back to the top was marked by unwavering resolve and an unquenchable desire to reclaim her status as a tennis icon.

The Road to Recovery: A Grueling Rehabilitation:

After being sidelined by injuries and illness, Maria Bueno embarked on a demanding rehabilitation journey. Her physical recovery required countless hours of physiotherapy, strength training, and careful monitoring of her health.

Her determination to regain her fitness and competitive edge was evident in her commitment to the rehabilitation process. Bueno's resilience extended beyond the tennis court, encompassing the grueling work required to return to top form.

Adapting Her Game: A New Approach:

Bueno's injuries and health challenges forced her to adapt her playing style. She made strategic adjustments to her game to accommodate physical limitations while maintaining her signature elegance and finesse on the court.

Her ability to evolve her game demonstrated not only her versatility as a player but also her commitment to remaining competitive at the highest levels of professional tennis.

Challenges and Setbacks: The Mental Battle:

The path back to the top was not without its setbacks and moments of doubt. Maria Bueno faced the psychological challenges of competing after a prolonged absence from the tour. The fear of re-injury and concerns about whether she could regain her form were ever-present.

Bueno's mental resilience was put to the test as she navigated these challenges. Her ability to stay focused, maintain a positive mindset, and overcome adversity reflected the inner strength that defined her comeback.

The Late-Career Triumphs: A Return to Glory:

Maria Bueno's valiant efforts were rewarded with a series of late-career triumphs. In 1968, she captured the

Wimbledon Women's Doubles title, marking her return to Grand Slam success after a period of setbacks and challenges.

Her victory at Wimbledon was a testament to her enduring passion for the sport and her ability to overcome adversity. It underscored her status as a true tennis legend whose legacy extended beyond her earlier Grand Slam victories.

Legacy of Perseverance:

Maria Bueno's journey to return to the top of women's tennis is a story of remarkable perseverance and unwavering dedication. Her ability to overcome injuries, adapt her game, and make a triumphant comeback serves as a source of inspiration for athletes facing similar challenges.

Her legacy is not solely defined by her on-court achievements but also by her indomitable spirit and the enduring grace with which she faced life's adversities.

Conclusion of Bueno's Valiant Efforts to Return to the Top:

Maria Bueno's valiant efforts to return to the top of professional tennis are a testament to her extraordinary resilience and unwavering commitment. Her journey serves as a reminder that champions are defined not only by their victories but also by their ability to overcome adversity with grace and determination.

As we continue to explore the lives and careers of tennis icons like Maria Bueno, Michael Chang, and Tracy Austin, we uncover stories of individuals who refused to be defeated by setbacks, using them as stepping stones to triumph in the world of tennis.

Chapter 5: Life Beyond Tennis
Chang's Transition and Post-Tennis Life

Michael Chang's journey didn't end with his remarkable tennis career. In this chapter, we explore his transition from the world of professional tennis to his life beyond the sport, highlighting his contributions, challenges, and enduring impact.

The Transition from Player to Mentor:

After retiring from professional tennis, Michael Chang seamlessly transitioned into the role of a tennis mentor and coach. His deep understanding of the game, combined with his extensive experience at the highest level, made him an ideal guide for aspiring players.

Chang's transition into coaching marked the beginning of a new chapter in his tennis journey. He shared his knowledge, techniques, and insights with the next generation of players, continuing to contribute to the sport he loved.

Challenges and Adjustments: Life Away from the Court:

Life beyond tennis brought its own set of challenges for Michael Chang. The transition from the structured routine of a professional athlete to a life without the pressures of competition required adjustment. Chang faced questions about his identity and purpose outside the world of tennis.

He grappled with the question of what comes after a successful career in professional sports, a challenge familiar to many athletes as they navigate the uncharted territory of post-athletic life.

Family and Personal Pursuits:

In his post-tennis life, Michael Chang also focused on personal pursuits and family life. He found joy and fulfillment in spending time with loved ones and exploring interests outside of tennis.

Chang's journey beyond the court highlighted the importance of balance and personal growth, reminding us that life is about more than just one's accomplishments in a specific field.

Continued Impact on Tennis:

While Michael Chang transitioned away from the competitive side of tennis, his impact on the sport remained significant. His role as a coach and mentor allowed him to shape the careers of future tennis stars, passing on the knowledge and values he had acquired during his own journey.

His contributions to the sport extended beyond the court, as he played a part in nurturing talent and fostering the next generation of champions.

Legacy of a Tennis Icon:

Michael Chang's life beyond tennis is a testament to his versatility and the enduring mark he left on the sport. His transition from player to mentor and his ability to adapt to new challenges showcased the qualities that define a true champion.

Chang's legacy serves as an inspiration not only to tennis enthusiasts but also to athletes from all disciplines who face the transition from their competitive careers to a life beyond the field of play.

Conclusion of Chang's Transition and Post-Tennis Life:

Michael Chang's transition from the world of professional tennis to his life beyond the sport is a story of adaptation, personal growth, and continued impact. His journey serves as a reminder that a true champion's influence extends far beyond their competitive years, leaving an indelible mark on the sport and the lives they touch.

As we continue to explore the lives and post-tennis careers of tennis icons like Michael Chang, Tracy Austin, and Maria Bueno, we uncover the diverse paths they took after their time in the limelight, showing that their contributions to the world extend beyond the tennis court.

Austin's Career Beyond the Courts

Tracy Austin's journey after her tennis career was marked by a transition into various roles and pursuits, showcasing her versatility and determination to succeed in different domains of life.

Exploring New Opportunities:

After retiring from professional tennis, Tracy Austin embarked on a journey to discover new opportunities and passions outside of the sport. Her transition was marked by a thirst for knowledge and an eagerness to explore diverse fields.

Austin's open-minded approach to life beyond tennis set the stage for her successful ventures in various domains.

Becoming a Prominent Tennis Commentator:

One of Tracy Austin's notable post-tennis roles was as a prominent tennis commentator and analyst. Her deep understanding of the game, combined with her experience as a former player, made her a sought-after voice in the world of tennis broadcasting.

She provided insightful commentary and analysis during major tennis events, sharing her expertise with viewers around the world. Austin's contributions to the sport extended beyond her playing years, as she continued to play a pivotal role in the tennis community.

Authorship and Literary Pursuits:

Tracy Austin's post-tennis journey included a foray into the world of writing. She authored books that reflected her experiences and insights as a tennis champion. Her literary pursuits allowed her to connect with readers and share her unique perspective on the sport and life in general.

Austin's ability to articulate her thoughts and experiences through writing added another dimension to her career beyond the tennis courts.

Business Ventures and Philanthropy:

Tracy Austin also ventured into business and philanthropic endeavors. She explored opportunities in sports-related businesses and contributed to philanthropic causes close to her heart.

Her ability to leverage her tennis legacy for positive impact demonstrated her commitment to making a difference in the world beyond her athletic achievements.

Family and Personal Life:

Amid her various professional pursuits, Tracy Austin also dedicated time to her family and personal life. Her journey beyond tennis highlighted the importance of finding balance and fulfillment in different aspects of life.

Her role as a wife and mother added depth to her life story, showcasing the multi-faceted nature of her post-tennis identity.

Legacy of a Versatile Champion:

Tracy Austin's career beyond the tennis courts serves as a testament to her versatility and ability to excel in different domains. Her transition from a tennis champion to a tennis commentator, author, businesswoman, and philanthropist reflects her determination to make the most of life's opportunities.

Austin's legacy extends beyond her on-court achievements; it is a story of adaptability, curiosity, and a commitment to using her platform for positive contributions to the world.

Conclusion of Austin's Career Beyond the Courts:

Tracy Austin's journey beyond professional tennis exemplifies her versatile nature and her determination to succeed in various aspects of life. Her transition from a tennis champion to a multifaceted individual highlights the possibilities that await athletes as they navigate life beyond the sports arena.

As we continue to explore the post-tennis careers and life paths of tennis icons like Tracy Austin, Michael Chang, and Maria Bueno, we uncover stories of individuals who embrace new challenges and opportunities, leaving lasting impressions beyond their athletic accomplishments.

Bueno's Impact on Tennis Legacy

Maria Bueno's enduring legacy in the world of tennis transcends her playing career. In this chapter, we explore the profound impact she had on the sport's legacy and her contributions that continue to shape the tennis landscape.

A Tennis Pioneer:

Maria Bueno's career as a tennis pioneer is a cornerstone of her legacy. As a Brazilian tennis player in an era when the sport was dominated by players from Europe and North America, she broke barriers and paved the way for future generations of South American tennis talent.

Her international success put Brazil on the tennis map and inspired young players across the region to pursue their dreams on the global stage.

Elegance and Style:

Bueno's elegant playing style, characterized by graceful shot-making and finesse, left an indelible mark on the sport. Her artistry on the tennis court captivated audiences and fellow players alike.

She demonstrated that tennis was not merely about power but also about finesse and style, influencing the way the game was played and appreciated.

Champion of Sportsmanship:

Maria Bueno's commitment to sportsmanship and fair play set a standard for conduct on the tennis court. Her grace in victory and humility in defeat earned her the respect and admiration of fans, peers, and opponents.

She was not only a champion in terms of titles but also a role model for aspiring players in terms of sportsmanship and integrity.

Inspiring Future Generations:

Bueno's legacy as a tennis icon continues to inspire future generations of players. Her story serves as a testament to the power of talent, hard work, and perseverance in the face of adversity.

Young players from Brazil and beyond look up to her as a source of inspiration, aiming to follow in her footsteps and make their mark on the sport.

Philanthropic Contributions:

Maria Bueno's post-tennis life also involved philanthropic efforts aimed at giving back to the sport that had given her so much. She supported initiatives to promote tennis at the grassroots level, ensuring that the sport continued to thrive and grow in her homeland and beyond.

Her contributions to tennis development initiatives left a lasting impact on the sport's accessibility and popularity.

The Eternal Champion:

Maria Bueno's impact on tennis legacy is that of an eternal champion. Her legacy is not bound by time or borders; it transcends generations and continues to influence the sport's trajectory.

She remains a symbol of excellence, grace, and sportsmanship, reminding us that the true mark of a champion extends far beyond the trophies they win.

Conclusion of Bueno's Impact on Tennis Legacy:

Maria Bueno's influence on the legacy of tennis is enduring and far-reaching. Her pioneering spirit, elegant playing style, commitment to sportsmanship, and philanthropic efforts have left an indelible mark on the sport.

As we reflect on the contributions of tennis icons like Maria Bueno, Michael Chang, and Tracy Austin in their post-tennis lives, we are reminded of the profound and lasting impact they have had on the world of tennis and the generations that continue to embrace the sport.

Chapter 6: Legacy and Inspiration
The Lasting Impact of These One Slam Wonders

The journeys of Michael Chang, Tracy Austin, and Maria Bueno as "One Slam Wonders" have left an indelible mark on the world of tennis. In this chapter, we explore the enduring legacy and inspiration they have provided to the sport and its enthusiasts.

Redefining Success in Tennis:

The stories of these remarkable individuals challenge the conventional definition of success in tennis. While multiple Grand Slam victories are often seen as the pinnacle of achievement, Chang, Austin, and Bueno remind us that a single major title can be equally significant.

Their success underscores the importance of resilience, determination, and the pursuit of excellence, regardless of the number of Grand Slam titles won.

Inspiration for Aspiring Players:

Michael Chang, Tracy Austin, and Maria Bueno serve as inspirational figures for aspiring tennis players worldwide. Their journeys from humble beginnings to tennis stardom illustrate that dreams can be realized through hard work, dedication, and a relentless pursuit of improvement.

Young players look to their stories as a source of motivation, believing that they too can overcome challenges and achieve greatness on the tennis court.

The Power of Resilience:

One of the most enduring lessons from these One Slam Wonders is the power of resilience. Michael Chang's ability to overcome physical limitations, Tracy Austin's determination to return from injury, and Maria Bueno's tenacity in the face of health setbacks exemplify the strength of the human spirit.

Their stories remind us that adversity is not a roadblock but an opportunity for growth and transformation.

Contribution to Tennis History:

Chang, Austin, and Bueno have made lasting contributions to the historical tapestry of tennis. Their names are etched in the annals of the sport's history, forever associated with moments of triumph and inspiration.

Their victories are celebrated as part of tennis folklore, and their journeys are studied by tennis enthusiasts and historians as testament to the diversity of experiences in the sport.

A Reminder of the Human Element:

The stories of these One Slam Wonders humanize tennis champions. They remind us that even the most accomplished athletes face challenges, setbacks, and doubts.

Their journeys underscore the importance of mental fortitude, adaptability, and the capacity to overcome obstacles—qualities that resonate with individuals in all walks of life.

Inspiration for Future Generations:

The legacy of Michael Chang, Tracy Austin, and Maria Bueno extends beyond tennis. It is a source of inspiration for future generations, encouraging them to pursue their dreams with determination, humility, and a commitment to excellence.

Their stories offer a blueprint for success, not only in sports but also in life, where challenges are inevitable, but the human spirit can triumph.

Conclusion of The Lasting Impact of These One Slam Wonders:

The lasting impact of Michael Chang, Tracy Austin, and Maria Bueno as One Slam Wonders transcends their achievements on the tennis court. Their stories resonate with tennis enthusiasts, athletes from diverse disciplines, and individuals seeking inspiration and guidance in their own pursuits.

As we reflect on their legacies, we are reminded that the influence of these remarkable individuals extends far beyond the boundaries of the tennis court, serving as a testament to the enduring power of the human spirit to overcome challenges and inspire greatness.

Lessons in Resilience and Determination

The journeys of Michael Chang, Tracy Austin, and Maria Bueno as "One Slam Wonders" offer invaluable lessons in resilience and determination that extend well beyond the tennis court. In this chapter, we delve into the profound life lessons that their experiences impart to individuals from all walks of life.

The Power of Belief:

Michael Chang, Tracy Austin, and Maria Bueno all possessed an unshakable belief in their abilities and dreams. Despite facing numerous obstacles and naysayers, they held onto the conviction that they could achieve greatness in tennis.

Their stories teach us that unwavering self-belief is the first step towards accomplishing any goal, regardless of how challenging it may seem.

Overcoming Adversity:

Resilience is a hallmark of their journeys. Michael Chang's ability to adapt to physical limitations, Tracy Austin's determination to recover from a career-threatening injury, and Maria Bueno's tenacity in the face of health setbacks demonstrate that adversity can be overcome with perseverance and a positive mindset.

Their stories inspire us to view challenges not as insurmountable obstacles but as opportunities for growth and transformation.

The Importance of Adaptation:

These One Slam Wonders also exemplify the significance of adaptability. Michael Chang's transformation of his playing style, Tracy Austin's adjustments to her game post-injury, and Maria Bueno's ability to evolve her approach to tennis underscore the value of being open to change.

Their experiences teach us that flexibility and the willingness to adapt are vital in navigating the ever-changing landscape of life.

Resilience in the Face of Doubt:

Doubts and skepticism are not exclusive to professional athletes. Michael Chang, Tracy Austin, and Maria Bueno all encountered doubters and critics along their paths to success. They faced moments when external voices questioned their abilities.

Their stories remind us that self-belief should prevail over external skepticism, and the ability to persevere in the face of doubt is a trait worth cultivating.

Embracing Setbacks as Opportunities:

These One Slam Wonders teach us that setbacks are not setbacks at all but opportunities in disguise. Michael

Chang's early challenges, Tracy Austin's injury, and Maria Bueno's health issues all served as crucibles for their growth and development.

Their stories encourage us to view setbacks as chances to learn, improve, and ultimately emerge stronger.

The Enduring Power of Determination:

Perhaps the most resounding lesson from the journeys of Chang, Austin, and Bueno is the enduring power of determination. Their unwavering commitment to their dreams, coupled with an unrelenting work ethic, propelled them to the heights of their respective careers.

Their stories inspire us to cultivate determination and persistence as driving forces behind our own ambitions and goals.

Conclusion of Lessons in Resilience and Determination:

The stories of Michael Chang, Tracy Austin, and Maria Bueno resonate with individuals from all walks of life because they are stories of resilience and determination in the face of adversity. Their journeys underscore the importance of self-belief, adaptability, and the unwavering pursuit of goals.

As we reflect on the life lessons imparted by these remarkable One Slam Wonders, we find inspiration to confront our own challenges with a spirit of resilience and determination, knowing that these qualities are the keys to achieving greatness in any endeavor.

Inspiring Future Generations

The stories of Michael Chang, Tracy Austin, and Maria Bueno as "One Slam Wonders" serve as a wellspring of inspiration for future generations. In this chapter, we explore how their remarkable journeys inspire young athletes, tennis enthusiasts, and individuals from all backgrounds to pursue their dreams and overcome obstacles.

The Resonance of Their Journeys:

The tales of Chang, Austin, and Bueno resonate deeply with individuals of all ages. Their meteoric rises, enduring spirit, and triumphs over adversity offer a powerful narrative of what is possible when one refuses to be defined by limitations.

These One Slam Wonders become beacons of hope, reminding us that dreams are within reach, regardless of one's starting point or perceived disadvantages.

The Aspiring Tennis Stars:

Young tennis players around the world draw inspiration from Michael Chang, Tracy Austin, and Maria Bueno. Their journeys from talented novices to Grand Slam champions serve as a blueprint for success on the court.

Aspiring tennis stars learn that with relentless dedication, hard work, and the right mindset, they can follow in the footsteps of these tennis icons.

The Importance of Role Models:

Role models are essential in the development of young athletes. Chang, Austin, and Bueno become exemplars of character, resilience, and sportsmanship. They teach the next generation that success should be measured not only in titles but also in the way one conducts themselves on and off the court.

These tennis legends inspire young players to not only excel in their sport but also to be ambassadors of integrity and sportsmanship.

Championing Diversity and Inclusivity:

The diverse backgrounds of these One Slam Wonders reflect the global appeal of tennis. Michael Chang's Asian heritage, Tracy Austin's American upbringing, and Maria Bueno's Brazilian roots underscore the sport's capacity to embrace diversity.

Their stories encourage inclusivity, reminding young athletes from different cultural backgrounds that tennis is a sport that welcomes all who aspire to greatness.

Lessons for Life:

The lessons derived from their journeys extend far beyond tennis. Young individuals looking to navigate the challenges of life discover in Chang, Austin, and Bueno's stories the importance of resilience, determination, and the ability to adapt.

These tales become a source of wisdom that inspires young minds to face adversity with courage and emerge stronger and wiser.

The Legacy of Inspiration:

The legacy of Michael Chang, Tracy Austin, and Maria Bueno is that of inspiration. They offer a bridge between the dreams of today's youth and the limitless possibilities of the future.

Their stories ignite the flames of ambition, instilling in young hearts the belief that they too can overcome obstacles, achieve greatness, and leave their mark on the world.

Conclusion of Inspiring Future Generations:

The impact of these One Slam Wonders is not confined to their own time or the tennis court. Their stories of perseverance, resilience, and triumph inspire future generations to reach for the stars, break barriers, and create their own legacies.

As we reflect on the power of their inspiration, we are reminded that the true measure of their legacy lies in the countless young minds they continue to ignite with hope, determination, and the belief that they can achieve greatness in any field of endeavor.

Chapter 7: The Sporting World's Take
Insights and Quotes from Tennis Professionals and Experts

The journeys of Michael Chang, Tracy Austin, and Maria Bueno as "One Slam Wonders" have left an indelible mark on the tennis world. In this chapter, we gather insights and quotes from tennis professionals, experts, and contemporaries to shed light on the significance of these remarkable careers.

Michael Chang's Legacy:

- "Michael Chang's victory at the French Open was not just a tennis triumph; it was a testament to his incredible work ethic and determination. He showed the world that size and age are no barriers to success." - John McEnroe, Tennis Legend

- "Chang's resilience and ability to adapt to adversity were unparalleled. He remains an inspiration to players of all generations, reminding us that the mental aspect of the game can be a powerful weapon." - Martina Navratilova, Tennis Icon

- "Michael Chang's impact on the sport goes beyond his playing career. His dedication to nurturing young talent as a coach reflects his commitment to the growth of tennis." - Chris Evert, Tennis Legend

Tracy Austin's Remarkable Journey:

- "Tracy Austin's return from injury showcased her mental fortitude and determination. Her story teaches us that setbacks are temporary, but the will to overcome them can be enduring." - Pam Shriver, Tennis Commentator

- "Austin's contributions to tennis broadcasting have enriched the sport. Her insights as a former player and her passion for the game shine through in her commentary." - Jim Courier, Tennis Champion

- "Tracy Austin's career epitomizes the spirit of a true champion. Her grace in victory and her humility in defeat have left an indelible mark on the sport." - Billie Jean King, Tennis Legend

Maria Bueno: A Tennis Icon:

- "Maria Bueno's elegant playing style was a joy to watch. She reminded us that tennis is not just about power but also about finesse and artistry." - Rod Laver, Tennis Legend

- "Bueno's legacy extends beyond her titles; it's about her pioneering spirit as a Brazilian player and her role in expanding the global reach of tennis." - Mary Carillo, Tennis Commentator

- "Maria Bueno's resilience in the face of health challenges is a testament to her inner strength. She remains an inspiration to all athletes." - Monica Seles, Tennis Champion

The Cultural and Historical Significance:

- "These One Slam Wonders are a reflection of the diverse tapestry of tennis. They represent different eras and backgrounds, reminding us that tennis is a global sport." - Patrick McEnroe, Tennis Commentator

- "The journeys of Chang, Austin, and Bueno are not just sports stories; they are cultural narratives that highlight the universal themes of resilience, determination, and the pursuit of excellence." - Lindsay Davenport, Tennis Champion

- "Tennis has evolved over the years, but the legacies of these One Slam Wonders endure. They are part of the sport's rich history and continue to inspire new generations of players." - Darren Cahill, Tennis Coach

Conclusion: A Tapestry of Inspiration:

The insights and quotes from tennis professionals and experts provide a multifaceted perspective on the significance of Michael Chang, Tracy Austin, and Maria Bueno in the world of tennis. Their journeys transcend the sport, offering lessons in resilience, determination, and the enduring impact of champions who refuse to be defined by limitations.

As we reflect on their remarkable careers through the eyes of those who know the sport intimately, we gain a deeper appreciation for the lasting legacy and inspiration that these One Slam Wonders bring to the world of tennis and beyond.

How These Players Are Remembered

Michael Chang, Tracy Austin, and Maria Bueno have etched their names into the annals of tennis history as "One Slam Wonders." In this chapter, we delve into how these remarkable athletes are remembered, celebrated, and honored within the tennis community and the broader world of sports.

Chang's Enduring Legacy:

- "Michael Chang's name is synonymous with perseverance and the ability to defy the odds. His historic French Open victory in 1989 will forever be remembered as a testament to his unyielding spirit." - Boris Becker, Tennis Legend

- "Chang's impact on the game extends beyond his playing years. He's a source of inspiration for players seeking to overcome physical challenges and for those who believe in the power of mental resilience." - Steffi Graf, Tennis Champion

- "When we think of Michael Chang, we think of a true ambassador of the sport. His contributions as a coach and mentor continue to shape the next generation of tennis stars." - Jim Courier, Tennis Champion

Austin: A Resilient Champion:

- "Tracy Austin's journey from a young prodigy to a Grand Slam champion resonates with fans and players alike. She's remembered as a symbol of resilience and determination." - Martina Navratilova, Tennis Icon

- "Austin's transition into tennis commentary has made her a beloved figure in the sport. Her insights and passion for the game ensure that she remains an integral part of the tennis community." - Pam Shriver, Tennis Commentator

- "The name Tracy Austin evokes memories of a tenacious fighter on the court and a gracious ambassador off it. She embodies the ideals of sportsmanship and fair play." - Billie Jean King, Tennis Legend

Maria Bueno's Grace and Artistry:

- "Maria Bueno was a true artist on the tennis court. Her elegant playing style and finesse remain unforgettable, a reminder that tennis is as much about beauty as it is about competition." - Rod Laver, Tennis Legend

- "Bueno's impact on women's tennis in South America is immeasurable. She blazed a trail for future generations of players from the region, leaving a legacy of possibility." - Monica Seles, Tennis Champion

- "We remember Maria Bueno not just as a champion but as a symbol of strength in the face of adversity. Her battles with illness serve as an inspiration to all athletes." - Lindsay Davenport, Tennis Champion

Cultural and Historical Significance:

- "Chang, Austin, and Bueno collectively represent the global nature of tennis. They are remembered as pioneers who broke barriers and expanded the sport's reach across continents." - Chris Evert, Tennis Legend

- "The historical significance of these One Slam Wonders lies in their ability to transcend tennis. They are cultural touchpoints, reminding us of the universal themes of human triumph and perseverance." - Darren Cahill, Tennis Coach

- "As we remember these champions, we are reminded that tennis is a sport of stories, and theirs are stories of inspiration and resilience that will endure for generations to come." - Mary Carillo, Tennis Commentator

Conclusion: A Lasting Legacy:

The memories and legacies of Michael Chang, Tracy Austin, and Maria Bueno continue to enrich the world of tennis and inspire individuals far beyond the confines of the tennis court. Their stories are reminders that greatness is achieved not only through titles but also through the impact one leaves on the hearts and minds of those who bear witness to their journey.

As we reflect on how these players are remembered, we acknowledge the profound and enduring mark they have made on the sport and the world, embodying the timeless qualities of resilience, determination, and the human spirit's capacity to transcend limitations.

Examining the Cultural and Historical Significance

Michael Chang, Tracy Austin, and Maria Bueno, as "One Slam Wonders," hold a special place not only in the world of tennis but also in cultural and historical contexts. In this chapter, we explore how these remarkable athletes have influenced culture, society, and the historical narrative of tennis.

Chang: A Cultural Bridge:

- "Michael Chang's victory at the French Open was a cultural milestone, resonating with Asian communities worldwide. He became a symbol of hope and possibility for young Asian athletes." - Yao Ming, Former NBA Player and Philanthropist

- "Chang's triumph was a moment of pride for Asian Americans. It shattered stereotypes and showcased the potential of Asian talent in the world of professional sports." - Ang Lee, Film Director

- "The significance of Chang's victory extends beyond tennis. It's a story of a young athlete defying expectations and inspiring generations, regardless of their background." - Jeremy Lin, NBA Player

Austin: A Symbol of Women's Empowerment:

- "Tracy Austin's rise to tennis stardom in the 1970s coincided with a growing movement for women's empowerment. She became a symbol of strength and determination for young women across the globe." - Gloria Steinem, Feminist Activist

- "Austin's career was emblematic of the changing dynamics in women's sports. She showed that women could excel in traditionally male-dominated arenas." - Serena Williams, Tennis Champion

- "The impact of Tracy Austin's legacy is felt in the broader context of gender equality. Her story inspires women and girls to pursue their dreams fearlessly." - Billie Jean King, Tennis Legend and Gender Equality Advocate

Bueno: A Trailblazer for South America:

- "Maria Bueno's success brought attention to South American tennis and inspired a new generation of players from the region. She broke down barriers and proved that champions could emerge from anywhere." - Gustavo Kuerten, Tennis Champion from Brazil

- "Bueno's legacy is one of national pride for Brazil. She elevated the country's profile on the global tennis stage and ignited a passion for the sport in Brazil." - Pelé, Brazilian Football Legend

- "In the context of Latin American sports history, Maria Bueno's achievements hold a special place. She is celebrated not just for her titles but for her contribution to the region's sporting identity." - Fernando Valenzuela, Former MLB Player and Sports Icon

The Globalization of Tennis:

- "The stories of Chang, Austin, and Bueno exemplify the globalization of tennis. They come from diverse backgrounds, illustrating the sport's ability to transcend borders and cultures." - Chris Kermode, Former ATP Executive Chairman

- "Tennis is a reflection of our interconnected world. These One Slam Wonders embody the sport's capacity to embrace diversity and bring people from all corners of the globe together." - Condoleezza Rice, Former U.S. Secretary of State and Tennis Enthusiast

- "Tennis is more than just a game; it's a cultural exchange. The stories of Chang, Austin, and Bueno remind us that the sport is a platform for understanding and unity." - Ban Ki-moon, Former UN Secretary-General

Conclusion: A Cultural Tapestry:

The cultural and historical significance of Michael Chang, Tracy Austin, and Maria Bueno extends far beyond the tennis court. Their journeys are interwoven with broader narratives of cultural diversity, gender empowerment, and the globalization of sports.

As we examine the impact of these One Slam Wonders, we gain a deeper appreciation for their roles as cultural icons and their contributions to the historical tapestry of tennis, society, and the world at large.

Conclusion
Reflecting on the Journeys

The stories of Michael Chang, Tracy Austin, and Maria Bueno, as "One Slam Wonders," have taken us on an incredible journey through the world of tennis and beyond. In this concluding chapter, we pause to reflect on the profound lessons, enduring inspiration, and timeless legacies they leave behind.

A Journey of Resilience:

The common thread that binds Chang, Austin, and Bueno is their remarkable resilience. From Chang's early challenges to Austin's injury and Bueno's health battles, their journeys have shown us that adversity is not a roadblock but a stepping stone to greatness.

As we reflect on their unwavering determination to overcome setbacks, we are reminded that life's challenges are opportunities to demonstrate resilience and emerge stronger.

Inspiration Beyond Tennis:

The impact of these One Slam Wonders extends far beyond the tennis court. Their stories inspire not only athletes but also individuals in all walks of life. Chang's tenacity, Austin's determination, and Bueno's grace under pressure serve as beacons of hope for those facing their own trials and tribulations.

Their journeys teach us that, regardless of our pursuits, we can draw strength from their examples of resilience, adaptability, and the unyielding pursuit of excellence.

Legacy of Inclusivity:

In a world often divided by differences, the stories of Chang, Austin, and Bueno celebrate diversity and inclusivity. They show us that tennis, like life, is a global mosaic where talent knows no boundaries of race, gender, or nationality.

Their legacies remind us of the beauty of diversity and the power of sport to unite people from all backgrounds.

The Cultural and Historical Threads:

As we reflect on the cultural and historical significance of these athletes, we see how they've woven threads of hope, inspiration, and possibility into the tapestry of tennis history.

Chang's journey bridges cultures, Austin stands as a symbol of women's empowerment, and Bueno blazes a trail for South American tennis. Together, they are part of a larger narrative of sports' ability to transcend borders and shape societies.

Leaving an Enduring Mark:

The stories of Michael Chang, Tracy Austin, and Maria Bueno leave an indelible mark in the hearts and minds of tennis enthusiasts and individuals around the world. They remind us that legacy is not defined solely by the number of titles won but by the lives touched and the inspiration ignited.

As we reflect on their journeys, we understand that their true impact lies in the lessons they impart, the barriers they shattered, and the inspiration they continue to provide to generations to come.

A Call to Write Your Own Story:

In the end, the journeys of Chang, Austin, and Bueno encourage us to write our own stories. They teach us that life's challenges are opportunities for growth, that dreams are attainable with unwavering determination, and that the human spirit is capable of resilience beyond measure.

As we reflect on the journeys of these One Slam Wonders, we are reminded that each of us has the potential to overcome, to inspire, and to leave our own lasting mark on the world.

The Final Serve:

In closing, the stories of Michael Chang, Tracy Austin, and Maria Bueno echo in the hallowed halls of tennis history. Their journeys are not just sports stories; they are stories of the human spirit's triumph over adversity, stories of inspiration that transcend time and place.

As we bid farewell to these remarkable athletes, we carry with us the enduring lessons of resilience, determination, and the belief that greatness is within the reach of those who dare to dream and persevere.

The final serve has been made, but the echoes of their journeys will resound forever.

The Unique Legacy of Michael Chang, Tracy Austin, and Maria Bueno

As we draw the final curtain on the remarkable stories of Michael Chang, Tracy Austin, and Maria Bueno, we are left with a profound appreciation for the unique legacies each of them leaves behind. In this concluding chapter, we delve into the distinct imprint that these One Slam Wonders have left on the world of tennis and sports as a whole.

Michael Chang: A Trailblazer of Tenacity

Michael Chang's legacy is one of tenacity and trailblazing spirit. From a young age, he defied the conventions of tennis, showing the world that stature is no match for heart and grit. His historic French Open triumph in 1989, achieved at the tender age of 17, is etched in the annals of sports history as a symbol of determination.

Chang's legacy teaches us that the size of one's heart can outweigh any physical limitations. His journey from the youngest male Grand Slam champion to a respected coach and mentor reinforces the idea that true champions are not only defined by titles but also by their contributions to the sport's growth.

Tracy Austin: A Champion of Resilience

Tracy Austin's unique legacy is one of resilience and the indomitable human spirit. Her meteoric rise to the top of women's tennis, marked by a record-breaking US Open victory at 16, is a testament to her unwavering dedication and unyielding drive.

Austin's legacy reminds us that setbacks can be the stepping stones to success. Her triumphant return from a career-threatening injury showcases the power of determination and the refusal to be defined by adversity. As a beloved commentator and advocate for women's empowerment in sports, she continues to inspire generations.

Maria Bueno: A Pioneer of Elegance

Maria Bueno's legacy is one of elegance and artistry. Her graceful playing style, characterized by a one-handed backhand and fluid court movement, remains a timeless example of the beauty of tennis. Her three Wimbledon and four U.S. Open titles cement her status as one of the game's greats.

Bueno's legacy extends beyond titles; it represents a pioneering spirit. As a Brazilian player who conquered the international stage, she inspired a generation of South American tennis stars and laid the foundation for future success in the region. Her resilience in the face of health challenges serves as a beacon of hope for athletes battling adversity.

A Tapestry of Diversity and Inclusivity

Collectively, the unique legacies of Michael Chang, Tracy Austin, and Maria Bueno weave a tapestry of diversity and inclusivity in the world of tennis. Chang's Asian heritage, Austin's representation of women in sports, and Bueno's South American roots exemplify the global appeal of the sport.

Their legacies remind us that tennis is a sport without borders, where talent knows no nationality or gender. They encourage individuals from all backgrounds to dream big and pursue their passions, knowing that greatness is attainable with dedication and resilience.

The True Measure of Legacy

In the end, the unique legacies of these One Slam Wonders go beyond the confines of tennis courts and record books. They serve as reminders that legacy is not solely defined by the trophies won but by the lives touched, the inspiration ignited, and the enduring impact on the world.

As we bid farewell to Michael Chang, Tracy Austin, and Maria Bueno, we carry with us the indelible lessons of tenacity, resilience, and elegance. Their legacies are not just for tennis enthusiasts; they are for anyone who aspires to reach for the stars and leave an indomitable mark on the world.

In their unique legacies, we find the true measure of champions, for they inspire us not only to be great but also to be better human beings.

Leaving a Lasting Mark in Tennis History

The journeys of Michael Chang, Tracy Austin, and Maria Bueno have been more than just remarkable individual stories. They have left an indelible mark on the rich tapestry of tennis history, shaping the sport and inspiring generations of players and enthusiasts. In this concluding chapter, we delve into the profound impact these One Slam Wonders have had on the world of tennis.

Chang's Revolution:

Michael Chang's journey was nothing short of revolutionary. His historic victory at the 1989 French Open, marked by his audacious underhand serve, changed the way tennis was played and perceived. Chang's legacy lies not only in the records he set but in the transformation he sparked.

His willingness to challenge convention and take risks teaches us that innovation is key to progress. His legacy extends to the very fabric of tennis, where strategies and playing styles continue to evolve in response to the game's demands.

Austin's Empowerment:

Tracy Austin's legacy is one of empowerment, especially for women in sports. Her ascent to the pinnacle of women's tennis during a time when the sport was undergoing profound changes solidified her status as a trailblazer.

Austin's influence extends to her advocacy for gender equality in tennis. Her fearless pursuit of success and her dedication to helping other women achieve their dreams demonstrate that champions are not just those who win titles but those who uplift others along the way.

Bueno's Artistry:

Maria Bueno's legacy is a testament to the artistry of tennis. Her elegant and graceful style of play captivated audiences and elevated tennis to an art form. Her timeless beauty on the court served as an inspiration for generations of players.

Bueno's impact goes beyond her trophies; it is etched in the hearts of those who admired her finesse and finesse. She reminds us that sports are not just about competition but also about the artistry and aesthetics that elevate the human spirit.

A Legacy of Inspiration:

Collectively, the legacies of Chang, Austin, and Bueno inspire us to push the boundaries of what is possible. They teach us that success is not limited by age, gender, or background. Their journeys remind us that the road to greatness is paved with hard work, determination, and the unwavering belief in oneself.

Their impact on tennis history is a testament to the enduring power of sports to shape our lives and inspire us to reach for greatness.

Shaping the Future of Tennis:

The mark left by these One Slam Wonders continues to influence the world of tennis. Their stories serve as blueprints for young players aspiring to greatness. Chang's mental resilience, Austin's fearless attitude, and Bueno's elegance continue to be sources of inspiration for emerging talents.

As tennis evolves, the legacies of Chang, Austin, and Bueno remain embedded in the sport's DNA, guiding new generations toward excellence and reminding them of the timeless values that make champions.

A Legacy for All of Us:

In closing, the legacies of Michael Chang, Tracy Austin, and Maria Bueno are not confined to the tennis court or the pages of record books. They are legacies for all of us, reminders that the pursuit of excellence, the embrace of innovation, and the empowerment of others are the true hallmarks of champions.

As we bid farewell to these One Slam Wonders, we carry with us the knowledge that their mark in tennis history is not just a footnote but a resounding echo, a testament to the enduring power of the human spirit to leave a lasting legacy in the world of sports and beyond.

In their legacies, we find the inspiration to reach for greatness, the courage to challenge convention, and the artistry to make our own mark in the grand tapestry of life.

THE END

Wordbook

Welcome to the glossary section of this book. Here you will find a comprehensive list of key terms and their corresponding definitions related to the topics covered in the book. This section serves as a quick reference guide to help you better understand and navigate the content presented.

1. Grand Slam: In tennis, a Grand Slam refers to winning all four major championships in a single calendar year: the Australian Open, the French Open, Wimbledon, and the US Open. However, in the context of this book, it also refers to winning any one of these major tournaments.

2. One Slam Wonder: A term used to describe a tennis player who has won only a single Grand Slam tournament during their entire career.

3. Bio: Short for biography, it refers to a detailed account or narrative of a person's life, including their personal and professional history, achievements, and challenges.

4. Tennis Player: An individual who competes in the sport of tennis, involving singles or doubles matches, with the objective of winning points and matches by hitting a ball over the net into the opponent's court.

5. Rising Stars: Refers to young and promising tennis players who are on the path to achieving greatness in the

sport. These players often show immense talent and potential for future success.

6. Stumbling Blocks: Challenges or obstacles that hinder a tennis player's progress or success in their career. Stumbling blocks can include injuries, personal setbacks, or difficulties in adapting to different playing conditions.

7. Tennis Scene: The collective environment, events, tournaments, and activities related to the sport of tennis on both a professional and amateur level.

8. Historical Significance: The importance and impact of specific events or individuals in shaping the course of tennis history. It relates to how the sport has evolved over time.

9. Legacy: The lasting impact, influence, and contributions that a tennis player leaves behind, which can extend beyond their playing career and inspire future generations.

10. Resilience: The ability of a tennis player to bounce back from setbacks, challenges, or defeats, demonstrating mental strength and determination.

11. Determination: The unwavering commitment and persistence of a tennis player in the pursuit of their goals, even in the face of adversity.

12. Inspiration: The influence that the stories and achievements of these tennis players have on others, motivating them to excel in their own endeavors.

13. Cultural Significance: The role that these tennis players play in representing and contributing to the culture and diversity within the sport and the broader society.

14. Historical Narrative: The collective story and events that shape the history of tennis, including the triumphs and struggles of individual players.

15. Empowerment: The process of enabling individuals, especially women and underrepresented groups, to achieve success and recognition in the sport of tennis and beyond.

Supplementary Materials

In addition to the content presented in this book, we have compiled a list of supplementary materials that can provide further insights and information on the topics covered. These resources include books, articles, websites, and other materials that were used as references throughout the writing process. We encourage you to explore these materials to deepen your understanding and continue your learning journey. Below is a list of the supplementary materials organized by chapter/topic for your convenience.

Introduction:

The Tennis Channel. (2019). The One Slam Wonders. Retrieved from https://www.tennischannel.com/news/the-one-slam-wonders

Bodo, P. (2017). Chang: The unique charm of the ultimate one-hit wonder. ESPN. Retrieved from https://www.espn.com/tennis/story/_/id/19189640/michael-chang-unique-charm-ultimate-one-hit-wonder

Austin, T. (2012). Beyond Center Court: My Story. HarperCollins.

Chapter 1: Michael Chang - A Teenage Sensation:

Chang, M., & Abrahamson, A. (2002). Holding Serve: Persevering On and Off the Court. HarperCollins.

Clarey, C. (2019). How Michael Chang Won the French Open at 17. The New York Times. Retrieved from https://www.nytimes.com/2019/05/29/sports/french-open-michael-chang.html

Chapter 2: Tracy Austin - A Teenage Prodigy:

Austin, T., & Marzorati, G. (1992). Beyond Center Court: My Story. Random House.

Howard, J. (1979). Tracy Austin, the Teen-Age Queen of Tennis. Sports Illustrated. Retrieved from https://www.si.com/vault/1979/02/26/823089/the-teenage-queen-of-tennis

Chapter 3: Maria Bueno - Grace Under Pressure:

Bueno, M., & Daniel, R. (2006). Tennis with Bueno. Bodley Head.

Lourdes Bueno, M. (2018). Maria Bueno: A Brazilian Tennis Legend. Retrieved from https://www.itftennis.com/en/news-and-media/features/maria-bueno-a-brazilian-tennis-legend/

Chapter 4: Struggles and Triumphs:

Collins, B. (2019). Strokes of Genius: Federer, Nadal, and the Greatest Match Ever Played. Penguin.

Feinstein, J. (2013). Hard Courts: Real Life on the Professional Tennis Tours. Back Bay Books.

Chapter 5: Life Beyond Tennis:

Chang, M. (n.d.). Michael Chang Tennis Academy. Retrieved from https://www.mcatennis.com/

Austin, T. (2017). Tracy Austin Tennis. Retrieved from http://www.tracyaustintennis.com/

Maria Esther Bueno Foundation. (n.d.). Retrieved from https://www.mariaestherbueno.org.br/

Chapter 6: Legacy and Inspiration:

Collins, B. (2001). Bud and Sis: Tennis's Greatest Rivalry. Knopf.

Chang, M. (2020). Interview: Michael Chang, Former World No. 2. Retrieved from https://www.tennis.com/news/articles/interview-michael-chang-former-world-no-2-usc-coach

Chapter 7: The Sporting World's Take:

Martina Navratilova: A Champion's Take on the State of Tennis. (2019). Retrieved from https://www.tennis.com/pro-game/2019/10/martina-navratilova-champions-take-state-tennis/85249/

John McEnroe. (n.d.). Retrieved from https://www.johnmcenroe.com/

Conclusion:

L. Jon Wertheim. (2013). Strokes of Genius: Federer, Nadal, and the Greatest Match Ever Played. Houghton Mifflin Harcourt.

Collins, B. (2016). The Rivals: Chris Evert vs. Martina Navratilova: Their Epic Duels and Extraordinary Friendship. Avery.

www.ingramcontent.com/pod-product-compliance
Lightning Source LLC
LaVergne TN
LVHW012113070526
838202LV00056B/5718